GREAT MOMENTS IN
HOCKEY

by James Buckley Jr.

WORLD ALMANAC® LIBRARY

Please visit our web site at: www.worldalmanaclibrary.com
For a free color catalog describing World Almanac® Library's
list of high-quality books and multimedia programs,
call 1-800-848-2928 (USA) or 1-800-387-3178 (Canada).
World Almanac® Library's fax: (414) 332-3567.

Library of Congress Cataloging-in-Publication Data

Buckley, James, Jr.
    Great moments in hockey / by James Buckley, Jr. —— North American ed.
        p. cm. —— (Great moments in sports)
    Summary: Recounts ten high points in the history of hockey, including the 1942 Stanley
Cup win for the Toronto Maple Leafs, the 1980 Olympic gold medal game between the
United States and Russia, and the career of Hall of Famer Mario Lemieux.
    Includes bibliographical references and index.
    ISBN 0-8368-5347-4 (lib. bdg.)
    ISBN 0-8368-5361-X (softcover)
    1. Hockey—Canada—History—Juvenile literature. 2. Hockey—United States—
History—Juvenile literature. [1. Hockey—History.] I. Title. II. Great moments in
sports (Milwaukee, Wis.)
    GV847.25.B83 2002
    796.962—dc21   2002016850

This North American edition first published in 2002 by
World Almanac® Library
330 West Olive Street, Suite 100
Milwaukee, WI 53212 USA

This U.S. edition © 2002 by World Almanac® Library.

An Editorial Directions book
Editor: Lucia Raatma
Photo researcher: Image Select International Ltd.
Copy editor: Melissa McDaniel
Proofreader: Sarah De Capua
Indexer: Tim Griffin
Art direction, design, and page production: The Design Lab
World Almanac® Library editorial direction: Mark J. Sachner
World Almanac® Library art direction: Tammy Gruenewald
World Almanac® Library production: Susan Ashley and Jessica L. Yanke

Photographs ©: Getty Images, cover; Joe Traver/NCAA, 3; Getty Images, 5; Hockey Hall
of Fame, 7, 8, 8; Getty Images, 9; Hockey Hall of Fame, 10, 11; Getty Images, 12, 13, 14;
Hockey Hall of Fame, 15; Corbis, 16, 17; Getty Images, 18; Corbis, 19; Hockey Hall of
Fame, 20; Getty Images, 21, 22, 23, 24; Corbis, 25; Hockey Hall of Fame, 26, 27, 28;
Corbis, 29; Hockey Hall of Fame, 30, 32; Reuters/Popperfoto, 33 top, 33 bottom; Getty
Images, 34; Corbis, 36; Getty Images, 37 left; Corbis, 37 right; Getty Images, 38, 39, 40,
41; Joe Traver/NCAA, 42, 43, 44, 45, 46 top; Corbis, 46 bottom.

Opposite: *Krys Kolanos hits the ice and follows the puck
into the crease after his dramatic, game-winning goal
clinches the 2001 NCAA championship for Boston
College. The University of North Dakota had staged a
stirring comeback in regulation time, but BC wasted
little time during the overtime period to put the
game—and the national championship—on ice.*

Contents

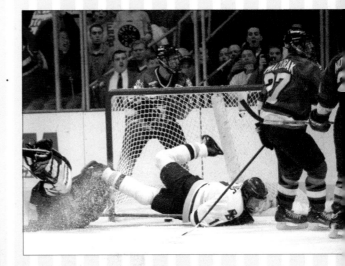

Introduction

Ever since people figured out how to move around on ice without falling down every other step, they have played games on lakes, ponds, and rivers covered with the hard, white stuff.

Scandinavian countries played many varieties of stick-and-ball games, whacking the ball back and forth while wearing crude skates or rough shoes that held a grip on the ice. As skating technology improved, the games became more organized, with several varieties of what would become hockey developing in Canada and some northern European countries.

The key point in the development of hockey as an organized sport was the introduction of indoor ice rinks. The ability to create a consistent, level field of ice in a restricted space gave rise to the game fans recognize today as ice hockey. While today's modern, high-tech arenas (some of which can convert from a basketball court to an ice hockey rink in just a few hours) are a far cry from old-time wooden floors covered with pipes that froze a thin layer of water, the game remains the same blend of speed, power, and stamina it has always been.

By the 1920s, the National Hockey League (NHL) had established itself as the best brand of hockey played in the world. Canadians dominated the game, but Americans played a big part, too. Around the world, European and Russian teams played in their own leagues, and everyone got together at the Olympics every four years.

In the history of the NHL, the Olympics and other international competitions, and U.S. college hockey, dozens of great players, games, championships, and moments stand out. All of these moments combine the fast-moving excitement that is big-time hockey with the thrill of seeing athletes strive to reach the top in their sport, no matter what the odds.

In this book, you'll relive ten of the greatest of those moments. Some come from the NHL's early days, when players were so rough and tough that goalies played without face masks. Other moments are from more recent years in the

A goal's-eye view of the action between the Toronto Maple Leafs and the Montreal Canadiens. These two teams, along with the Detroit Red Wings, Boston Bruins, New York Rangers, and Chicago Blackhawks, make up the "Original Six"—the legendary clubs that provided the early National Hockey League with the stability and exciting rivalries it needed to succeed between the 1940s and 1960s and lay the groundwork for the vastly expanded NHL that fans know today.

NHL, when better training methods and equipment, as well as the introduction of European players, have helped the game and its players reach new heights of skill, speed, and excitement. Add into this blend the indelible memories from the college hockey and international competition, and you've got a mix of stories that will be sure to keep a hockey fan warm all winter long.

The sport has come a long way from crude sticks, frozen ponds, and players in makeshift footwear, but thanks to those early pioneers, fans today can celebrate the fastest game on ice.

WILL THIS GAME NEVER END?

A Six-Overtime Thriller from Hockey's Early Days

Hockey games are scheduled for sixty minutes of play—three twenty-minute periods separated by fifteen-minute intermissions. It's a grueling game, but the players are in top shape, and they practice hard and often so that the rigors of the long game and the long season don't wear them out. But during one game early in NHL history, two teams' stamina was tested beyond what any team has gone through before or since.

Marathon Matchup

On March 24, 1936, the Detroit Red Wings and Montreal Maroons faced each other in the first game of their best-of-five semifinal series. The winner would advance to face the Toronto Maple Leafs in the 1936 Stanley Cup finals. The game was played in the Montreal Forum before ten thousand rabid Maroons fans. The atmosphere was tough for visiting teams and even tougher for the visiting goalie.

"When I went into the game, I had butterflies," said Red Wings goalie Normie Smith afterward. "As the game went on, I seemed to settle down. Of course, I had no idea it would go on so long."

After three periods of regulation, the two teams had played to a scoreless tie. To break the tie, the teams would return to the ice for a twenty-minute, sudden-death overtime period after a short intermission. The first team to score would win the game, but amazingly, the two teams would play into their sixth additional period before the outcome was decided. (In those days, overtimes were used only for playoff games. Regular-season games that ended in a tie remained a tie.)

Flying chips, 1930s-style: Red Wings rookie Modere "Mud" Bruneteau was rested and ready to play when he hit the ice during the sixth overtime period of the seemingly endless 1936 game between Detroit and the Montreal Maroons.

Neither team scored in the first three overtime periods. By this time, there had been two hours of play, and the effects of skating two complete games back-to-back began to show. Players' legs were tired, their jerseys were soaked with sweat, goaltenders' pads weighed many pounds more than when they had started. The Maroons drank coffee and brandy to keep their strength up; the Red Wings went through two gallons of muscle-relaxing ointment. The players weren't the only ones feeling the effects of the long game, either. Fans began to tire just watch-ing the game, and even those staffers maintain-ing the ice rink had a hard job ahead of them.

"They only swept the ice [with brooms] between periods back then," remembered Detroit's Pete Kelly. "This was in the days before the Zamboni machine. The ice was very rough with skate marks and ruts. The longer the game went on, the more difficult it was to control the puck."

Overtime Number Six

Two more overtimes went by, still without any scoring, and fans were falling asleep in their

The Wings' Mud Bruneteau scored a goal eight minutes into the sixth overtime, finally ending the marathon on ice with the Maroons.

seats or leaving to get some sleep so they could get to work the next morning. At two o'clock in the morning on March 25, the teams came back onto the ice for the sixth overtime period. The Red Wings had a secret weapon, and they chose this period to unveil it. Rookie right wing Modere "Mud" Bruneteau had not played much during the season, scoring only two goals, and he had yet to play in this marathon game, so he was fresh and ready to go, while his teammates skated like zombies.

Detroit sent Mud out on the ice to shake things up midway through the sixth overtime. Mud did more than that. At about 2:25 in the morning, nearly eight minutes into the sixth OT period, Mud took a pass from Hec Kilrea and fired a shot that went over the sprawling Montreal goalie, Lorne Chabot, and into the net.

A team photo of the 1936 Detroit Red Wings.

The game—finally—was over.

Exhausted and spent, both teams fell to the ice. The Red Wings were too tired even to celebrate. Amazingly, the puck had stuck into the twine of the net and never did fall to the ice; perhaps it, too, was too tired to go on. Mud finally made his way off the ice, and excited but exhausted fans stuffed dollar bills into his jersey and glove in thanks for saving them from the seemingly endless game.

"Thank goodness Chabot fell down as I drove the puck into the net," Mud said. Chabot had stopped Detroit's first sixty-five shots, but number sixty-six was the game winner. Detroit goalie Normie Smith had gotten over his butter-flies well enough to stop an amazing ninety shots on goal without allowing a single one to get past him.

The six-OT game had lasted 176 minutes and 30 seconds, or nearly three complete games played back-to-back-to-back—still the longest game in NHL history. For the Red Wings, it was the start of something good. After winning the series against the Maroons, Detroit defeated Toronto three games to one to capture the team's first-ever Stanley Cup trophy.

Above: *The "Original Six" tradition of excellence lives on: Detroit standout defenseman Nicklas Lidstrom (5), left wing Brendan Shanahan (14), and 1994 MVP-winning center Sergei Federov (91) race for the puck in 2001.*

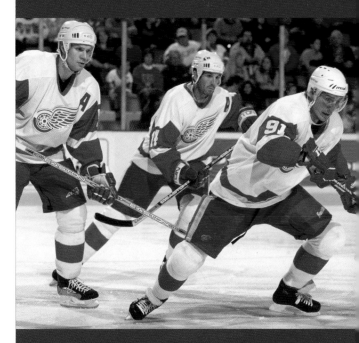

THE ORIGINAL SIX

The NHL was founded in 1917, and six teams have been a part of the league ever since. These six franchises became the bedrock that played on through lean years and strong years, and they were eventually joined by the many teams playing today. Their legacy is celebrated today in T-shirts, posters, and hats with the "Original Six" logo.

The Original Six franchises are:

Boston Bruins

Chicago Blackhawks

Detroit Red Wings

Montreal Canadiens*

New York Rangers

Toronto Maple Leafs

(*This is a different franchise from the Montreal Maroons that played in the six-OT game in 1936. The Maroons entered the NHL in 1924 and withdrew in 1938.)

THE ULTIMATE COMEBACK

The Toronto Maple Leafs Battle Back from a 3–0 Series

In a best-of-seven-game playoff series, falling behind two games to none means that your team will almost surely lose. Falling behind three games to none means that, statistically, the series is over. In all the sports that use seven-game playoffs, only a tiny handful of teams have ever come back from a 3–0 deficit to win the series. And only one team has done it in the finals of its sport's championship. That team was the Toronto Maple Leafs in 1942.

The 1942 Toronto Maple Leafs, the team that staged a legendary comeback in the Stanley Cup finals.

In this archival photo from 1942, the Toronto Maple Leafs celebrate a goal against Detroit at Maple Leaf Gardens.

Preventing the Sweep

Heading into those Stanley Cup finals, the Maple Leafs had a cloud of doom over their heads, having lost in the finals six times since winning the championship in 1932. But in 1942 they had finished with a much better record than the opposing Detroit Red Wings and were favored to win. After three games, however, that didn't look very likely. The Red Wings outscored the Leafs 12–6 and swept the first three contests.

Game 4 was played in Detroit, and the hometown fans packed their arena, hoping to see their Wings complete the sweep.

Toronto coach Hap Day benched his veteran players and inserted a lineup headed by rookies and younger players. Their youthful enthusiasm and fresh legs must have helped, because Toronto staved off elimination by coming back from being two goals down to win 4–3. But they still had a big hill to climb, down three games to one.

Back in Toronto for Game 5, the Leafs' young players continued to rally their team, with Don Metz notching a hat trick

An obviously exuberant Syl Apps, the captain of the Maple Leafs, accepts the 1942 Stanley Cup from NHL president Frank Calder.

games down in a series, and the flip side was true, too—no team had ever lost a series after being ahead three games to none.

Sealing It with Game Seven

The final game of the series was played in Toronto's Maple Leaf Gardens. After two periods, neither team had scored; it

in the Leafs' 9–2 romp. Still, every game could be the Leafs' last, with the Red Wings only one victory from triumphantly parading Lord Stanley's cup around the rink.

The series returned to Detroit for Game 6, and this time it was veteran goalkeeper Turk Broda who was the star of the game for Toronto. Broda turned back every Red Wings shot to post a clutch shutout. Stunned Detroit players and fans now faced what a few days earlier they had thought impossible—a Game 7 in which either team could win the championship. No NHL team had ever come back from being three

seemed as if no one wanted to win this vital game. Then Detroit took a 1–0 lead into the third period, and it looked as if their great collapse would end. But a power-play goal by Toronto's Sweeney Schriner tied the score. Minutes later, the come-from-behind Leafs scored again, with Pete Langelle doing the honors. Schriner added an insurance goal, and that was it. Toronto won the game 3–1, the series 4–3, the Stanley Cup (the first of five they would win in the 1940s), and a place in the record books as the only 0–3 comeback team in sports finals history.

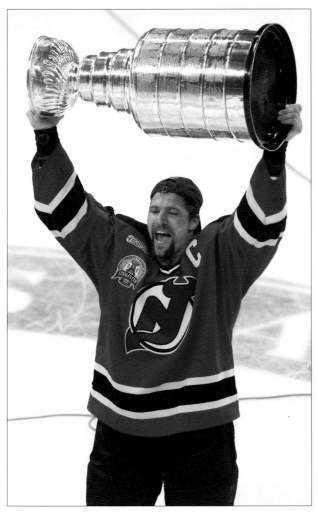

Scott Stevens of the New Jersey Devils parades across the ice with the 2000 Stanley Cup. Along the road to the cup, the Devils came back from a 1–3 deficit in the Eastern Conference finals.

OTHER COMEBACKS

Only one other team has come back from a 3–0 deficit during the Stanley Cup playoffs. In 1975, the New York Islanders were down by three games to the Pittsburgh Penguins in the Eastern Division quarterfinals. But the Islanders did the same thing the Maple Leafs did in 1942—they fought back to win the series. Unfortunately for Islander fans and others who had developed an attachment to this come-from-behind pack, New York lost in the next round of the playoffs and couldn't bring home the Cup as Toronto had done.

Fourteen teams have come back from 3–1 deficits in other rounds of the playoffs, including three in recent years:

2000: New Jersey came back from 3–1 to defeat Philadelphia in the Eastern Conference finals, on the Devils' way to the Stanley Cup title.

1999: St. Louis rallied from being down 3–1 to knock off the Phoenix Coyotes in a Western Conference quarterfinal.

1998: Edmonton was down 3–1 to Colorado but came back to defeat the Avalanche in a Western Conference quarterfinal.

HE SCORES . . . AND FLIES!

How Bobby Orr Changed the Game

Sports stories are often filled with huge statements that can be just a bit too big for reality. That kind of writing is called "hyperbole," and you hear it all the time: "Greatest game ever! Greatest series ever! Greatest player ever! Greatest franchise ever!"

In the case of Bobby Orr, however, saying that he was the greatest defender in NHL history and that he changed the way his sport is played is not hyperbole. By turning defenders into scorers, Orr made hockey more exciting than ever and helped propel the NHL to the tremendous popularity it enjoys today.

Boston's Bobby Orr, shown here against the Chicago Blackhawks, will long be remembered both as one of hockey's top defensemen and as one of the game's most exciting scorers.

On Offense and Defense

After he joined the NHL's Boston Bruins in 1966, Orr quickly changed the role of defenseman from one of staying back and letting the forwards attack to one of joining the attack. No NHL defenseman had scored twenty goals in more than twenty years; Orr topped that total in seven different seasons. He later led the league in scoring and assists, still the only defenseman ever to do so.

"When I saw Orr coming down on me, well, the first thing I did was to say a little prayer, if I had time," said Hall of Fame goalie Johnny Bower.

In the 1969–70 season, Orr had perhaps the greatest year of any player in NHL history. He was named the league's MVP, top defenseman, and playoffs MVP, and he was also the scoring leader. It was the only time that one player captured all four of those honors.

The capper to his amazing season was the Stanley Cup finals, in which the Bruins faced the St. Louis Blues. Boston won the first three games. Game 4 was tied 3–3 after regulation, and the two teams began overtime.

Orr ended things quickly.

Going Airborne

With only forty seconds gone in the first overtime period, he got the puck at St. Louis's blue line and skated in on goalie Glenn Hall. He faked

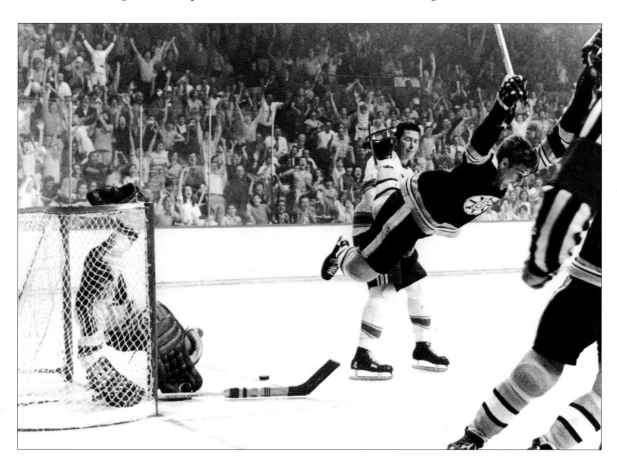

The Bruins' Bobby Orr is airborne after scoring the 1970 Stanley Cup–winning goal in overtime against St. Louis.

Hall down to the ice and flipped the puck in over the goalie's shoulder. Just as Orr finished his follow-through, an opponent hooked his skates, sending him flying through the air. But the goal stood and the Stanley Cup belonged to the Bruins for the first time since 1941.

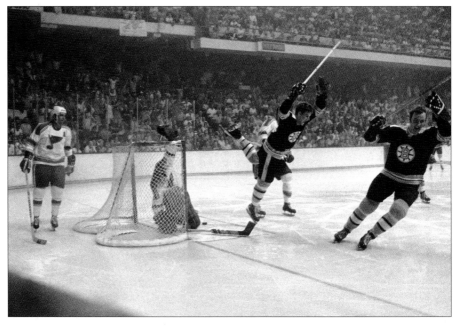

Back on his feet, Orr joins his teammates in celebrating his winning goal and the Bruins' Stanley Cup victory over the Blues.

A photograph of Orr just after the goal is the most famous shot in hockey history. It shows him about four feet in the air, his body face down and parallel to the ice, with both arms flung out in triumph and a yell of victory coming from his mouth as other players stand back in awe.

A Commendable Career

Orr continued his amazing play for eight more seasons, helping the Bruins win another cup in 1972. Opponent Rod Gilbert of the Rangers said after that championship, "One man is not supposed to be able to beat a

TOP DEFENSEMEN

The Norris Trophy is awarded annually to the NHL's top defenseman. Here are the players who have won the most Norris Trophies

Player, Team(s)	Norris Trophies
Bobby Orr, Boston Bruins	8
Doug Harvey, Montreal Canadiens/New York Rangers	7
Ray Bourque, Boston Bruins	5
Chris Chelios, Montreal Canadiens/Chicago Blackhawks	3
Dennis Potvin, New York Islanders	3
Paul Coffey, Edmonton Oilers/Detroit Red Wings	3
Pierre Pilote, Chicago Blackhawks	3

Bobby Orr (waving) and teammates John Adams (left), Don Marcote, and Bill Speer are mobbed during the Bruins' 1970 Stanley Cup victory parade in downtown Boston.

whole team!" But Orr practically did.

Knee injuries forced Orr's retirement in 1979. Although he had a relatively short career, his impact on the game is still felt today, as defensemen routinely score and are a big part of most teams' offenses.

"You can say some things about each of the great players," said Jacques Plante, another Hall of Fame goalie, "such as 'he's a good skater, or a good stickhandler, or he has a great shot,' but something is always missing. Bobby Orr has it all. He is the best I've seen—ever!"

OTHER OVERTIME CUP WINNERS

Besides Orr's, several other sudden-death-overtime goals have won Stanley Cups, including one that helped start one of hockey's great dynasties. In 1980, right wing Bobby Nystrom scored at 7:11 of the first overtime period in Game 6 to give the New York Islanders a victory over the Philadelphia Flyers. The Islanders won the next three Stanley Cups in a row, making June celebrations an annual event on Long Island.

Nystrom still pops a video of that game into the VCR once in a while and sits down with his family to relive that special moment.

"My son always asks me what it felt like to score the goal that won the Stanley Cup," he told *Sports Illustrated*. "And all I can say is that it was a dream come true. It was nice to give something to my teammates."

Here are ten other cup-winning goals scored in overtime since 1950:

2000: Jason Arnott, New Jersey Devils, Game 6

1999: Brett Hull, Dallas Stars, Game 6

1996: Uwe Krupp, Colorado Avalanche, Game 4

1977: Jacques Lemaire, Montreal Canadiens, Game 5

1970: Bobby Orr, Boston Bruins, Game 4

1966: Henri Richard, Montreal Canadiens, Game 6

1954: Tony Leswick, Detroit Red Wings, Game 7

1953: Elmer Lach, Montreal Canadiens, Game 5

1951: Bill Barilko, Toronto Maple Leafs, Game 5

1950: Pete Babando, Detroit Red Wings, Game 7

THE GOAL HEARD 'ROUND THE WORLD

Canada vs. the Soviet Union in a Different Cold War

Canada sees itself as the birthplace and international home of hockey. It is the most popular sport in the nation, more NHL players come from there than from any other country, and many Canadian kids learn to skate as soon as they can walk. One of the most popular shows on Canadian TV is the long-running *Hockey Night in Canada*. Featuring live games, highlights,

Phil Esposito played professionally in Boston for the Bruins, but he was proud to represent his native Canada in the 1972 "Summit Series" with the Soviet Union.

commentary, and news, the show has been on the air in one form or another since 1931. So in the 1960s, as Canada's national teams, made up of amateurs, began to lose regularly to powerful teams from the Soviet Union, the entire nation was disturbed.

Fans and players accused the Soviets of using professionals, or of giving amateur players jobs that let them spend all their time practicing and playing. In fact, Canada refused to play hockey in several Winter Olympics due to this very issue. They felt their amateur players would not match up fairly with the Soviet players.

The Summit Series

In 1972, the two nations finally put their best professional players on the ice for what was called the Summit Series. Four games were to be played in Canada and four more in the Soviet Union. It was seen by Canadians as a way to reclaim dominance of their "native" game.

Canada soon realized, however, that doing so would mean winning a tough fight. The initial four games were played in Canada, and the Soviets crushed the Canadians 7–3 in the first game. Canada came back to win and tie the next two games, but the Soviets won Game 4. The two teams headed to the Soviet Union with Canada trailing 2–1–1.

Canadian national heroes such as Phil Esposito, Yvan Cournoyer, and Ken Dryden were faced with traveling halfway around the world to defend their country's honor. The trip must have tired them out, because they lost the first game in Moscow. However, they bounced back to win the next two games. After seven grueling contests, the score was the Soviet Union 3, Canada 3, with 1 tie game.

"We were having a rough time in Moscow with the lousy hotels, phone calls to the players' rooms in the middle of the night, the Russians snatching much of the food we had sent over

Hockey Hall of Famer Yvan Cournoyer, shown here with the Montreal Canadiens, was one of Canada's conquering heroes in the Summit Series against the Soviets.

for the team . . . and the terrible officiating by the European officials," recalled coach Harry Sinden. "But a long cheer at the end of the first game in Moscow by the Canadian fans was a big lift for our spirits."

In fact, more than three thousand Canadians had made the long trip to cheer their team on. Strangely, Russian players felt that they gained no advantage by playing on their home ice. The fans who had cheered them on to victories in league play and other competitions were shut out of the Summit Series, because all the tickets went to government officials who were not nearly as loud in their support.

Final Battle in Moscow

The final game is etched on the collective memory of Canadian hockey fans. Reports at the time noted that nearly everyone in the country tuned in to watch or listen. Students listened in auditoriums after classes were suspended, and offices were bare as people left to tune in on their radios or watch on television.

After two periods, the score was 5–3 in

Team Canada forward Paul Henderson takes on two Soviets, one of them the goalie, in the Summit Series. Canadians recently voted his tie-breaking goal in Game 8 one of the most remembered—and revered—moments in Canadian sports history.

favor of the Soviet Union. A pair of Canadian goals tied the score at 5–5 midway through the third and final period. In a moment that lives forever in Canadian sports history, forward Paul Henderson corralled a rebound of an Esposito shot and sent the puck toward the Soviet goal with less than a minute to go in the game.

His shot was stopped at first by goalie Vladimir Tretiak, who himself would become one of the greatest players of all time. But Henderson took that rebound and zipped the puck past Tretiak for the game-winning goal with thirty-four seconds left. All of Canada cheered and soon welcomed home their conquering heroes.

In 1999, that 1972 squad was named the greatest team of the twentieth century in a poll conducted by the Hockey Hall of Fame. A huge crowd gathered near the hall to see the players reunited and to watch a sculpture be unveiled. The fans cheered, using the Russian words for "no" and "yes" in a chant they had invented in 1972: "Nyet, nyet, Soviet . . . Da, da, Canada!"

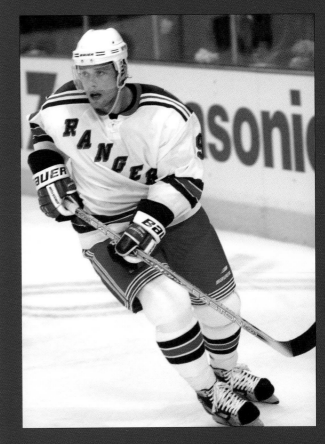

GREAT RUSSIAN STARS

Although they no longer dominate international hockey, Russian players still have a big impact on the sport. Since the breakup of the Soviet Union in the early 1990s, many players from Russia and other former Soviet states have joined the NHL. Among the best Russian players in today's NHL:

Pavel Bure (above), RW, New York Rangers

Sergei Federov, C, Detroit Red Wings

Nikolai Khabibulin, G, Tampa Bay Lightning

Viktor Kozlov, C, Florida Panthers

Igor Larionov, C, Detroit Red Wings

Alexander Mogilny, RW, Toronto Maple Leafs

Sandis Ozolinsh, D, Carolina Hurricanes

Alexei Yashin, C, New York Islanders

Sergei Zubov, D, Dallas Stars

THEY CALL HIM "MR. HOCKEY"

Gordie Howe Set Scoring Records Only Gretzky Could Break

In the 1940s, 1950s, and 1960s, a tough-as-nails, high-scoring Detroit Red Wings forward was consistently ranked as one of the NHL's top scorers and most valuable players. In the 1970s, a grandfather in his late forties made his mark in a new pro league—the World Hockey Association (WHA)—ranking among the WHA's top scorers and earning MVP honors.

The grandfather and the Red Wings forward were the same

Gordie Howe, shown here in an early publicity shot with the Detroit Red Wings, grew up on hockey and played professionally in the NHL and WHA over the course of five decades.

guy: Gordie Howe.

No hockey player has put in more ice time than the legendary Howe, whose powerful scoring touch helped him set all-time records for goals and scoring that stood until Wayne Gretzky came along more than thirty years later.

Setting Records

Howe grew up in Saskatchewan loving hockey and spending more time on the ice than in school. After a few seasons in the minors, he played his first NHL game at the age of eighteen in 1946. In a sign of things to come, he scored a goal in that first game.

In the 1949–50 season, he kicked his goal-scoring into high gear, finishing second in the league with thirty-five goals. Although Detroit won the Stanley Cup that year, they did so without Howe, who had been badly injured earlier in the playoffs. But Detroit fans showed how much they loved the hard-charging, high-scoring young player by demanding that he come out for a bow after the final game.

Howe in action with the Red Wings against the New York Islanders in March 1965.

The Red Wings won three more cups through 1955, while Howe continued to be among the league's scoring leaders. In all, he won six Art Ross Trophies, given to the league's top scorer, and he was named the league MVP six times. By 1960, he had become the NHL's all-time scoring leader, overtaking the famous Canadiens player Maurice "the Rocket" Richard.

Howe was a model of consistency, finishing in the top five in scoring for twenty years in a row. He played in twenty-nine All-Star games, and his record for games played (1,760) remains unchallenged.

Gordy Howe (right) is joined by his son Mark on the Heroes of Hockey team, part of the NHL All-Star game in 1999. With this promotional appearance, Gordy's appearances in a pro hockey uniform spanned six decades.

Back on the Ice

In 1971, Howe retired and took an executive position with the Red Wings, but life in a suit just didn't, well, suit him. In 1973, Howe, then forty-five, joined the Houston Aeros of the new World Hockey Association. Playing with him on the team were his sons, Mark and Marty, marking the first time that a father and sons had played on the same pro team in any sport.

The man they call "Mr. Hockey" showed that a couple of years away from the game

hadn't changed him. He was among the league's scoring leaders, and he won the MVP award in 1974—the same year that Mark was named Rookie of the Year. The Howes led the Aeros to a pair of WHA championships.

In 1977, Gordie and Marty moved to the New England Whalers, who played in Hartford, Connecticut. Two years later, the WHA folded, and several of its teams joined the NHL. One of them was the Whalers, so, amazingly, ten years after he last played in the NHL, Gordie Howe, hockey's all-time leading scorer at that time, triumphantly returned to the league that he had helped make famous.

Howe was a wonder. He turned fifty-two that season but still played a full eighty-game season, scoring goals and banging bodies with players less than half his age. He became a hero to senior sportsmen everywhere and a great example of how competitive fire and great talent can be put to good use no matter what the age of the body doing the playing. He finally retired for good in 1980 with stunning career totals of 801 goals and 1,850 points.

A Hockey Legend

Want the opinion of a real expert? Scotty Bowman is one of the most successful coaches in hockey history. He has more victories to his name than any other coach, and he's tied for most Stanley Cup titles with eight.

On Gordie Howe's Web site (www.mrhockey.com), Bowman says, "I pick Gordie as my #1 all-time player. He played the longest. He was the toughest player of his era. He was the best offensive player and defensively he was used in all situations. He could play center, right wing, defense. He could shoot right and he could shoot left. If you could make a mold for a hockey player it would be him. I never thought there was another player close to him."

Some of Howe's scoring records have fallen, mostly to Wayne Gretzky (see Chapter 8), for whom Howe was a boyhood idol. But Howe's record for durability, his impact on the game, and his importance to the sport and the NHL will never be forgotten.

HOCKEY OCTOPUS

In Detroit, fans of the Red Wings have a strange custom—sometimes during the playoffs, they throw an octopus onto the team's home ice during a game.

Why throw an eight-legged sea creature onto the ice?

The first creature made its appearance in 1952, when it took eight victories in the playoffs to win the Stanley Cup. Eight legs . . . eight wins. The tradition continued occasionally as the Red Wings won more cups.

When the team opened a new arena in 1979, an octopus made an appearance. And in 1995, a fifty-pound blob of octopus plopped onto the ice during the Eastern Conference finals.

Howe presents an award in 1984 to Edmonton Oiler Wayne Gretzky, the man who would go on to challenge Howe's records—and set a few of his own.

MIRACLE ON MANCHESTER

A Great Comeback for the Los Angeles Kings—and a Bigger Upset

On April 10, 1982, the 16,005 hockey fans who filled the Fabulous Forum at Manchester Avenue and Prairie Boulevard in Inglewood, California, thought they were just coming to an NHL playoff game. They saw more than that— they were treated to the single greatest comeback in the history of the National Hockey League.

Not even Hollywood could have scripted such an improbable ending to a game that forever will be known as the "Miracle on Manchester."

Paul Coffey, one of the superstars of the 1981–82 Edmonton Oilers—and future Hall of Famer.

Facing the Oilers

The visiting Edmonton Oilers were almost impossible to stop during the 1981–82 regular season and finished with a league-best record of 48–17–15. They were a brash, cocky collection of young superstars, led by future Hall of Famers Wayne Gretzky, Mark Messier, and Paul Coffey and backstopped by perennial All-Star goalie Grant Fuhr. They had scored a total of 417 goals that season, shattering a sixty-six-year-old NHL goal-scoring record. Not surprisingly, they entered the playoffs as the overwhelming Western Conference favorite, expected to challenge the defending champion New York Islanders for the Stanley Cup.

Meanwhile, the hometown Los Angeles Kings had slogged through yet another dismal year. The Oilers had trounced them a total of five times during the regular season, including an 11–4 shellacking in November and a 10–3 thumping in December. On January 11, 1982, the Kings had fired coach Parker McDonald and hired Don Perry, a minor-league coach.

Under Perry's guidance, the team finished the regular season with a very poor 24–41–15 record. Despite their abysmal record, the Kings still managed to make the playoffs at a time when sixteen of the twenty-one NHL teams qualified.

Because of the Oilers' dominance and the Kings' losing record, the hometown L.A. squad was a heavy underdog headed into their first-round, best-of-five series against the Oilers. Surprisingly, the two teams split the first two games in Edmonton, setting the stage for Game 3 in Los Angeles. Before a sell out crowd at the Forum, the two teams met to continue the series.

Edmonton came out quickly, taking a 5–0 lead after the first two periods, thanks to their record-setting goal scorers. They spent much of the evening skating circles around the Kings' defenders. During a particularly inept Kings effort on a second-period power play, the Kings were showered with boos from the home

In 1982, the Oilers' Mark Messier was also headed for the Hockey Hall of Fame, but that didn't seem to intimidate the underdog L.A. Kings.

crowd. Able to relax for the first time in the series, the Edmonton bench playfully joined the crowd in booing the Kings. This brief show of poor sportsmanship would soon come back to haunt the Oilers.

During the break before the third period, Kings coach Don Perry practically conceded defeat, telling his players to play well enough in the third to gain momentum for the next game. His team would soon do a lot more than that.

Not even the finesse of another future Hall of Famer, Edmonton's Wayne Gretzky, could prevent the amazing comeback of the Los Angeles Kings in the 1982 NHL playoffs.

top of the slot. Bozek swept the puck past a sprawled Grant Fuhr to tie the game, sending the Forum crowd into a frenzy. The elated Kings and dejected Oilers skated off the ice, amazingly tied 5–5 after regulation play.

During the intermission before the overtime, the Kings celebrated wildly in their locker room. Among them was Daryl Evans. Evans had spent most of the season in the minor leagues and was added to the playoff roster only at the last moment. The Kings would soon be glad they made that decision.

Third-Period Comeback

Early in the third period, defenseman Jay Wells finally got the Kings on the scoreboard, slapping the puck from the left point past Fuhr to make the score 5–1. Doug Smith, Charlie Simmer, and Mark Hardy also soon scored for the Kings, cutting the Oilers lead to 5–4. Suddenly, the rout was turning into a classic comeback.

With less than a minute to play, Kings goaltender Mario Lessard was pulled for an extra skater, and the Kings buzzed around the Edmonton net, desperately trying to score the tying goal. With five seconds left, the puck squirted to rookie Steve Bozek, stationed at the

Fantastic Finale

At 2:35 into overtime, there was a face-off to the right of Fuhr. Evans collected the puck and whacked it toward the net. The puck went over Fuhr's shoulder, crashed into the net, and the Kings' comeback was completed with a 6–5 victory.

The fans in the stands screamed at the top of their lungs, stunned and thrilled at what they had witnessed. On the ice, the Kings also erupted into a frenzied celebration, complete with a five-man dog pile that slid half the length of the ice. The dog pile eventually included the whole team, and they left behind sticks and other gear on the ice

Edmonton goalie Grant Fuhr in action.

that was still there when young Evans came out to enjoy a few more cheers.

"But it was almost like I floated through it," Evans, who now works as a radio analyst for the Kings, told the *Detroit News*. "I did two laps and I never touched a thing. I couldn't have done that again if I tried."

The Kings went on to complete a stunning five-game upset of the Oilers, continuing their miracle play by winning the deciding fifth game in Edmonton 7–4. But their victory in the series would long be overshadowed by their 6–5 Game 3 win—a triumph that would forever be remembered, thanks to the address of the arena in which the game was played, as the "Miracle on Manchester."

DYNASTIES

The Oilers didn't win the cup in 1982, but only a few years later they won four Stanley Cup titles in five seasons. Here are some of the top Stanley Cup championship dynasties.

Team	Years	Titles
Toronto Maple Leafs	1945–51	5 of 7
Toronto Maple Leafs	1947–49	3 in a row
Montreal Canadiens	1956–60	5 in a row
Montreal Canadiens	1965–73	7 of 9
Montreal Canadiens	1976–79	4 in a row
New York Islanders	1980–83	4 in a row
Edmonton Oilers	1984–90	5 of 7

QUADRUPLE OVERTIME

A Marathon Game Seven between the Capitals and the Islanders

Hockey is a hard game to play, hard on the body and hard on the mind. Players skate, check, shoot, and defend, putting their bodies on the line time and again in an atmosphere of ice and sweat. The intensity is amplified in the playoffs and reaches sky-high proportions in any Game 7 of a playoff series, when defeat means your season is over.

Hockey is such a tough game that most skaters are only on the ice for a couple

Capitals star Mike Gartner scored his team's first goal on April 18, 1987, and he later referred to that long night as "a bad dream you couldn't wake up from."

of minutes at a time before returning to the bench for a breather. They skate in shifts, as different lines of players change with their teammates on the fly, leaping over the sideboards to get right into the action.

In a normal sixty-minute hockey game, players can expect to get very tired, very sore, and very worn out. Now imagine playing two complete hockey games back-to-back . . . and doing so in the pressure cooker of a

Game 7. But that's just what happened on April 18, 1987.

A Game 7 Tie

The Washington Capitals had led the Eastern Conference semifinals three games to one over the New York Islanders, but the Isles had clawed back to tie it at three. Now, Game 7 at Washington's Capital Centre would decide it all. But after sixty minutes of hockey, nothing was decided. The game was tied 2–2, and all the fans in the arena stuck to their seats to root their Caps on to victory.

They were stuck there a long time. Through three complete twenty-minute overtime periods, to be exact. Over and over shots flew at each goalie, and over and over they were turned away. Midnight came and went, the concession stands ran out of food, broadcasters filled the time between periods interviewing each other, kids at the game fell asleep in their seats. But still, the two teams played on.

The referees let them play, not calling one penalty for the last eighty-nine minutes of the game. "It was like pond hockey," said Washington's Bobby Gould. "No one checked. You always had room to skate." But all that room didn't lead to any goals for the first three OTs.

Between periods, the players

NEW RULES FOR OVERTIME

For many years, overtime periods were played only in playoff games, while ties in the regular season were not broken. In the playoffs, overtime periods are twenty minutes long, and teams keep playing in overtime until someone scores. Beginning in the 1983–84 season, teams had been playing one five-minute, sudden-death overtime period if the game ended in a tie. The winner of this overtime period received two points in the standings, while the loser got one, since they had at least earned a regulation-time tie. If no one scored after that one overtime, the game would remain a tie.

In 1999, the NHL adopted a new set of rules governing overtime play during the regular season.

The new rules kept the five-minute period in place, but now each team sends out only four skaters, plus a goalie. It was hoped that having fewer players on the ice would help speed up the game, increase scoring chances, and give more teams victories. Also, teams now have four lines in the standings: one each for wins, losses, ties, and overtime victories.

New York Islander Pat LaFontaine, who scored the winning goal against the Washington Capitals in Game 7 of the 1987 Eastern Conference semifinals.

retreated to the locker room and collapsed. Some tried to sleep; others simply lay on the floor with their feet up.

Into the Fourth Overtime

The fourth overtime period started after 1:30 on Easter morning, Washington time. Now the fatigue was starting to show, and play was very ragged. Finally, as the remaining fans continued to shout themselves hoarse, the end came. New York's Pat LaFontaine fired a slap shot toward Capitals goalie Bob Mason, and the puck hit the metal upright of the net and banked in.

"I never saw it," Mason said. "I just heard it."

What the fans saw was the fifth-longest game in NHL history and the third longest since 1943. They also saw an exhausted Capitals team sit limply on the bench while the Islanders celebrated . . . slowly. Eventually, both teams met at center ice for the traditional post-series handshake.

Both teams played like warriors, never giving up until the last shot found the net. Capitals owner Abe Pollin put it best when he said, "It's a shame someone had to lose a game like that."

ON AND ON AND ON . . .

During the 2000 Stanley Cup playoffs, two very long games tested both players and fans. Game 4 of the Eastern Conference semifinals went to a fifth overtime before Keith Primeau of the Philadelphia Flyers scored to defeat the Pittsburgh Penguins 2–1.

In Game 5 of the Stanley Cup finals between the Dallas Stars and New Jersey Devils, the teams played three regulation periods and two overtime periods without either team scoring. In the third overtime, the Stars finally broke through with a goal to win the game. The Devils overcame this defeat, however, to come back and win the cup.

During the 1950 Stanley Cup finals, all five games in the series went to overtime, the only time that has ever happened. The Detroit Red Wings finally beat the New York Rangers to win the cup.

Above: *Keith Primeau of the Philadelphia Flyers scored the winning goal against the Pittsburgh Penguins to put an end to quintuple overtime in Game 4 of the 2000 Eastern Conference semifinals.*

Left: *Dallas Stars defenseman Dave Manson (left) checks New Jersey Devils winger Jay Pandolfo into the air and off the puck during the 2000 Stanley Cup finals.*

THE GREAT ONE'S GREATEST

A Look at Wayne Gretzky's Amazing Career

Some great hockey moments, such as the Miracle on Manchester, appear almost out of nowhere, suddenly and without warning, to make a permanent mark on the hockey world. Other moments can be seen coming from a long way away . . . but that does not make them any less special.

For most of his career, Wayne Gretzky, known simply as "The

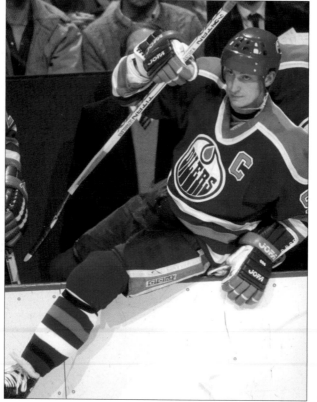

Wayne Gretzky, "The Great One," turned pro at age seventeen with the Edmonton Oilers of the World Hockey Association. In 1979, after the WHA had folded, both the Oilers and Gretzky moved to the NHL.

Great One," made a beeline toward many of hockey's greatest all-time career and single-season records. As he approached each of the marks—many of which were set by his boyhood idol, Gordie Howe—fans, opponents, broadcasters, and writers around the world followed his every step, counting down the goals, assists, and points he needed to add another line to his incredible record book.

He had a great role model in the record-setting Howe. "When I was a kid, I wanted to play, talk, shoot, walk, eat, laugh, and be like Gordie Howe," Gretzky wrote in his autobiography. "I once even went to the barbershop and asked for a haircut exactly like Gordie's, even down to the little bald spot at the top."

A Young Talent

The young man from Brantford, Ontario, had quickly established himself as one of hockey's great new talents when he scored a record 378 goals as a ten-year-old in junior hockey. At age seventeen, Gretzky turned pro in the World Hockey Association. He entered the NHL in 1979 when his team, the Edmonton Oilers, joined the older league. He soon pretty much owned the NHL, winning the Hart Trophy, which is given to the league's most valuable player, for eight straight seasons beginning in 1979–80.

Though not that big by hockey standards, standing only six feet tall and weighing about 160 pounds (73 kilograms), Gretzky was simply unstoppable on the ice. The records started falling early and they never stopped. In 1981, he scored fifty goals in only thirty-nine games, the fastest ever to that mark. The next year, he scored a single-season record of ninety-two goals, an average of more than one goal per game, and added 120 assists. He had 163 assists, another record, in 1985–86, and a total of 215

WAYNE'S NUMBERS

There is not enough room in this book to list all of Wayne Gretzky's achievements on the hockey rink. But here are some of the key career or single-season records that he still holds (through 2000–01 season):

Most goals, career: 894

Most goals, single season: 92 (1981–82)

Most assists, career: 1,962

Most assists, single season: 163 (1985–86)

Most points, career: 2,856

Most points, single season: 215 (1985–86)

Most seasons with 40+ goals: 12

Most seasons with 100+ points: 15

Most playoff goals: 122

Most playoff assists: 260

Most All-Star game goals: 13

Gretzky battles for the puck during a 1982 meeting with the New Jersey Devils.

points on the season (hockey points are given to players by adding goals and assists).

He led Edmonton to the first of its four Stanley Cup championships in 1984. After his four-year run, and more and more goals, Gretzky was traded to the Los Angeles Kings in 1988. In Los Angeles, he won another MVP trophy in 1989 and led the Kings to the Stanley Cup finals, while also winning two more scoring titles. In 1988, he achieved the first of his many career scoring

marks, becoming the NHL's all-time leader in assists.

Breaking Records

It was also with the Kings that he achieved two of his greatest personal statistical milestones. On October 15, 1989, Gretzky became the NHL's all-time leading scorer by notching his 1,851st point, again topping a mark held by Howe. Ironically, the point that broke the record came on a game-tying goal against his old team, the Oilers.

On March 23, 1994, Gretzky scored the 802nd goal of his career, breaking the record set, again, by Howe.

Amazingly, when he retired in 1999, Gretzky finished his career with 1,962 assists, meaning that even had he not scored a single goal in the NHL, he would still have been the all-time leader in points. As it was, his career total of 2,856 points is a record that seems unbreakable.

Gretzky was indeed The Great One.

In 1988, the talented Gretzky was traded to the Los Angeles Kings and went on to set a ton of scoring records.

MRS. GREAT ONE

Wayne's wife is Janet Jones, an American actress and dancer who has appeared in numerous movies and commercials. They first met in 1981 when Janet was dancing on an episode of a show called *Dance Fever*. Wayne wasn't dancing, though; he was a judge on the show, which used celebrities to choose the winners.

He didn't forget the beautiful, blonde Janet, however, and followed her career closely. They met again in 1987 and were married in 1988 in Edmonton, Alberta, Canada. Their wedding—the biggest in Canadian history—made news all over the world, and more than two hundred reporters came to the ceremony. Seven hundred guests also filled the church, including dozens of hockey stars, and more than ten thousand people stood outside to wish the newlyweds well.

Wayne and Janet have four children: Paulina, Ty, Trevor, and Tristan.

SUPER MARIO

How Mario Lemieux
Beat the Odds

The story of Mario Lemieux, the great center for the Pittsburgh Penguins, is so unbelievable that Hollywood moviemakers probably would refuse to put it on the screen, figuring no one would think it could possibly be real.

But it was . . . and it is.

A Hockey Life

Lemieux grew up in the suburbs of Montreal, in a family so hockey-crazy that they filled the base-ment of their house with ice so Mario and his brother could prac-tice skating indoors. Lemieux quickly

Mario Lemieux was named Rookie of the Year during his first season with the Pittsburgh Penguins.

became a star player and was the first pick of the 1984 NHL draft. The first time he touched the puck in an NHL game, he scored a goal, and he just kept scoring almost every time he laced up his skates. He was named Rookie of the Year, became an instant star, and quickly made the Penguins one of the league's top teams.

In 1987–88, he did the unthinkable, outscoring the great Wayne Gretzky to win the Art Ross Trophy. In 1988–89, he did it again, while also falling one point short of becoming the only player to join Gretzky in the 200-point-per-season club. Unfortunately, back injuries that would continue to plague Lemieux for the rest of his career began at this time, and he missed the start of the 1989–90 season.

But showing the amazing fortitude that is his hallmark, he bounced back from the hospital, won another scoring title, and led the Penguins to their first Stanley Cup championship. He scored thirty-four points in the playoffs, had five game-winning goals, and was named the playoffs MVP.

Facing Illness

After the Penguins repeated their championship in 1990-91, Lemieux just kept chugging along until doctors discovered a lump in his neck in 1992. The hockey world was stunned to learn that "Super Mario" had Hodgkin's disease, a

Lemieux showed what he was made of when he overcame Hodgkin's disease and back injuries to return to professional hockey in 2000.

Back on the ice in 2001, Lemieux takes on the New Jersey Devils in the Eastern Conference finals.

potentially fatal cancer of the lymph system. Fortunately, it was caught early and could be treated with radiation. To his doctors' and fans' amazement, Lemieux returned to the ice just days after his last treatment. While only playing sixty games (out of eighty) in that season, he won yet another scoring title.

The next two seasons were almost a complete loss, not to Hodgkin's but to back trouble. He returned to record two more great seasons, but his back pains proved to be too much. When he retired at age thirty-one after the 1997 season, he was the NHL's sixth all-time leading scorer. Lemieux is the only player ever to average more than two points per game. Because of his great record and the way injury cut his career short, Lemieux was elected to the Hockey Hall of Fame right away.

A Hockey Hero

Guess what? His story wasn't over yet. Lemieux put together a group of investors and bought the Penguins in 1999, helping to keep the struggling team in Pittsburgh. Mario had saved the Penguins again, but hockey's comeback king had yet another chapter to write.

In 2000, after more than three years away from the game, Lemieux decided to return to the ice and play. Being the team owner and a Hall of Famer meant he had no trouble making the team, and he proved that he had no trouble coming back yet again. In his first game back, he scored a goal and had two assists. His triumphant returns from disease, back injury, and retirement, along with his amazing goal-scoring abilities, have made Mario Lemieux one of hockey's greatest heroes.

LEMIEUX'S RECORDS

Mario Lemieux's amazing year-by-year record, which shows how many points he scored and how many times he came back

Year	Points
1984–85	100
1985–86	141
1986–87	107
1987–88	168
1988–89	199
1989–90	123
1990–91	45
1991–92	131
1992–93	169
1993–94	37
1994–95	did not play
1995–96	161
1996–97	122
2000–01	76

Lemieux (center) and the rest of Team Canada show off their 2002 Olympic gold medals, which they won by defeating Team USA in the 2002 Winter Games at Salt Lake City.

A COLLEGE CLINCHER

The Eagles Fly High

The National Hockey League is not the only venue for exciting ice hockey action. For more than fifty years, the annual NCAA Ice Hockey Championship has provided dozens of great stories and memorable moments.

The championship tournament has all the high-speed, hard-hitting action you expect to find in hockey, but it also includes the joy, spirit, and desire of young players, many of whom have professional dreams dancing through their

University of North Dakota goalie Karl Goehring aggressively defends the goal in the 2001 NCAA championship game against Boston College.

helmets. The players work very hard during the school year, combining class work with practice and games, often missing out on many social events to hone their skills on the rink.

Most of the top schools are found in the Northeast and Midwest, not surprisingly, since winter sports aren't too popular in the Sun Belt or out West. The chart on page 45 lists some of the top schools in NCAA tournament history. One of those schools, the University of North Dakota, found itself in a dogfight during the final game of the 2001 NCAA tournament. Its opponent was Boston College (BC), a school that hadn't won the title since 1949; North Dakota had won seven titles in that time.

Looking for a Title

Boston College had had a run of terrible luck in recent NCAA tournaments. In 1998, the Eagles lost the title game in double overtime to Michigan. In 1999, another overtime loss, this time to Maine, knocked them out in the semifinals. And in 2000, they had lost to this same North Dakota team in the finals.

Boston College forward Mike Lephart bears down on the puck against North Dakota.

"We were so close to grabbing that title," Coach Jerry York said. "It was hard to see it just disappear in an eyeblink. It really helped our mental toughness."

In the rematch of the 2000 final, the two teams played outstanding defense, but BC was just a little better, building a 2–0 lead with five minutes left to go. It seemed as if the Golden Eagles' curse would finally be lifted, but the veteran North Dakota team never gave up.

With just over four minutes left, BC was penalized and North Dakota received a power play. They made it even more of a power play by pulling their goalie, a risky move that put an extra man on the ice but left their goal open, which could have sealed their fate. Instead, it paid off as the two-man advantage turned into a goal. A little more than two minutes later, North

BC's Krys Kolanos scores the game-winning goal against a sprawling Karl Goehring.

Dakota's goalie again skated off and in the furious scramble in front of the BC net, Wes Dorey deflected a teammate's shot into the net, tying the game with just thirty-six seconds to go.

Breaking the Tie

"Our first reaction was, 'I can't believe this is happening again,'" said BC's Mike Lephart.

The fans at the rink in Albany, New York, site of the game, were thrilled by this tension-filled atmosphere as the sudden-death overtime started. North Dakota's amazing comeback had energized the entire arena.

But the end came quickly, and the Eagles lifted their tournament curse. With almost five minutes of sudden-death overtime gone, BC's Krys Kolanos beat North Dakota goalie Karl Goehring with a forehand shot that won the game and the NCAA title, adding another page to the long list of great college hockey moments.

Kolanos (11) joins a BC teammate in a victory dance following his dramatic goal.

SCHOOLS WITH MOST NCAA HOCKEY TOURNAMENT CHAMPIONSHIPS		
School	**Titles**	**Most Recent**
Michigan	9	1998
North Dakota	7	2000
Denver	5	1969
Wisconsin	5	1990
Boston University	4	1995
Lake Superior State	3	1994
Michigan Tech	3	1975
Minnesota	3	1979

Hockey Time Line

1860 A puck is first used in the game that is evolving into modern ice hockey; previously, players used a ball.

1885 After slowly evolving from a variety of icy games developed in Scandanavia and Scotland, hockey's first organized league is formed in Canada.

1892 Lord Stanley, the governor general of Canada, donates a silver trophy topped by a large cup, to be presented to the top hockey team in Canada. Today, the Stanley Cup is the oldest trophy in pro sports.

1917 The National Hockey League is founded in Toronto.

1920 Ice hockey joins the Winter Olympics.

1923 Teams shrink from seven players to six.

1940 The first pro hockey game is televised in the United States and Canada.

1947 The first NHL All-Star Game is played.

1955 The Zamboni machine, which cleans and resurfaces the ice between periods, is introduced to the NHL.

1967 The NHL doubles its number of franchises, adding six new teams to the "Original Six."

1976 Detroit's "enforcer," Dan Maloney, is put on trial for assault after an on-ice fight with another player. The public attention, many believe, resulted in a gradual decline in fighting in hockey. There still is fighting in hockey today but dramatically less than in years past.

1979 Four teams from the defunct World Hockey Association join the NHL.

1980 All-time great Gordie Howe plays with his sons Mark and Marty on the NHL's Hartford Whalers. Gordie is fifty-two years old at the time; the U.S. Olympic hockey team stages the "Miracle on Ice" by beating the Soviet team and going on to win the gold medal at the Winter Games in Lake Placid, New York.

1988 Wayne Gretzky is traded to the Los Angeles Kings. Gretzky's popularity exposes U.S. states in the West and Southwest to hockey in a much bigger way than ever before, and several expansion franchises are soon located in places like Colorado, Arizona, and San Jose, California.

1994 For the first time, pro players represent their nations at the Winter Olympics. In 1998, the NHL season stops for three weeks to allow players to travel to Nagano, Japan, to play in the Olympics.

1997 The NHL announces that it will expand to thirty teams by 2000, a goal the league succeeds in reaching.

1998 Women's hockey is introduced as a full medal sport in the Winter Olympics.

1999 Wayne Gretzky retires.

2002 At the Winter Olympics in Salt Lake City, Utah, Team Canada brings home the gold medal for the first time since 1952.

To Learn More

BOOKS

Adelson, Bruce. *Hat Trick Trivia: Secrets, Statistics, and Little-Known Facts about Hockey.* Minneapolis: Lerner, 1998.

Italia, Bob. *100 Unforgettable Moments in Pro Hockey.* Edina, Minn.: Abdo and Daughers, 1998.

Kramer, Sydelle A. *The Great Gretzky.* New York: Grosset & Dunlap, 2000.

McKinley, Michael. *The Magnificent One: The Story of Mario Lemieux.* New York: Grosset & Dunlap, 2002.

Muskat, Carrie L. *The Composite Guide to Hockey.* Broomall, Pa.: Chelsea House, 1998.

Sullivan, George. *All about Hockey.* New York: Putnam Juvenile, 1998.

INTERNET SITES

Hockey Hall of Fame
www.hhof.com
Official site of the Hockey Hall of Fame in London, Ontario, Canada.

Mr. Hockey
www.mrhockey.com
Gordie Howe's official Web site.

National Hockey League
www.nhl.com
Official site of the National Hockey League, with links to all the individual team sites.

NCAA Ice Hockey
www.ncaaicehockey.com
To read about great NCAA tournament games and see who has won the annual Hobey Baker Award, given to college hockey's top player.

USA Hockey
www.usahockey.com
Site of men's and women's national teams.

Index

ABOUT THE AUTHOR

James Buckley Jr. has written more than twenty sports books for young people on baseball, football, hockey, soccer, and the Olympics. He was an editor with Sports Illustrated *and the National Football League, where he helped start and wrote for nfl.com, superbowl.com, and Play Football, the NFL's official Web site for kids. He is the editorial director of the Shoreline Publishing Group, a book producer and editorial services company in Santa Barbara, California.*